HOLD TIGHT & REACH HARD

HOLD TIGHT & REACH HARD

Darrell Kane

Atlantic Way Publishing

Copyright © Darrell Kane 2020

All rights reserved. No part of this book may be reproduced in any form or by any electronic or mechanical means, including information storage and retrieval systems, without permission in writing from the publisher, except by reviewers, who may quote brief passages in a review.

If you share content from these pages on social media, please tag the author and mention the name of the book. If you did not pay for the book in your hands and it impacts you, please consider posting some reviews.[1]

Atlantic Way Publishing

Cover artwork by Nicola MacNeil
[1]Conscious statement by Vironika Wilde
Formatting by Mos_Designs
ISBN 978-0-9948423-0-5 (e-book)
ISBN 978-0-9948423-1-2 (paperback)

Table of Contents

PROLOGUE 5
TRICKLE.. 3
COMBAT 5
BEK 7
THE DIDN'T 9
ONE IN THE CHAMBER 13
EFFACE.. 17
TD1 19
DECIMATED 21
FRAGILITY 23
THE OTHER SHOE.. 25
THE ARENA 27
CAST DEEP 29
CYCLONE 31
STARS WANE 33
RANT 35
HEED THIS 37
FARROW AWAY... 39
HAD 41
IN SILENCE 43
END GAME... 45
THE 1 AND THE 3... 47
PIGGY BACK.. 49

TOMORROW	51
47th & EAU CLAIRE	53
HOLD TIGHT	61
WITH THANKS	63

The following was written by a happy person, disguised as a not so happy one.

PROLOGUE

All is intertwined,
Weaved together in a tight rope.

Smiles
Scowls
Hugs
Heartache

Broken hearts
Broken bones
First loves
First mistakes

Holding on
Letting go
Falling down
Getting up

Pride
Regret
Love
Sorrow

Loss

When it's quiet.

When it's dark.
When I'm lost in a moment
And no direction makes sense,
I pull on the threads.
Pull my experiences together.
Feel them wrap around me.
Warm me.
Lift me.

I remember I wouldn't be where I am right now without them...
And here isn't such a bad place to be.

TRICKLE

At that point,
It broke.

It was a slow trickle at first.
He stared at it intensely
At the risk of ignoring his surroundings.
But it wasn't a risk;
He ignored his surroundings.

He didn't notice the beauty of the bloom around the edges.
The clarity of the sand through the water.
The cresting of the sun.
The silence that wasn't uncomfortable.

The fixation was on what was not.

Insecurity did not promote security.
Romancing solitude did not enhance vows.
Disappearing into one's self did not complement unity.
An elevated state did not improve the every day,
Or stability,
Or selflessness.

At that point,
He broke.
"We need to talk," he said.
"I know," she said.

COMBAT

Maybe this is a way to combat it.

Get the heart rate up.
Step by step,
Stroke by stroke.
Nervous energy to positive exertion.
It certainly works,
If you can get out of bed.

Less time between inhales is
Less time for idle chatter.
Telling stories of places that never were,
Feelings that never happened,
And thoughts that didn't exist in reality.

Idle chatter cannot exist in reality
So it uses all the power of its volume and distractive force
To increase your heart rate and make your insides tingle,
But not from a good source.

It's not endorphins.
It's destruction.

Word by word,
Line by line,
Hoping you implode,
Crumble

Under the weight of your own undoing.
By focus, we feed it.
Unwittingly
But we do.

Maybe this is the way to combat it.

If you can only get out of bed.

BEK

He said what he was to say.

Gradually,
It diminished
To a whisper.

His larynx failed him.

Communication became
A system of grunts
And head nods.

The body atrophied.

No use of his arms.
No use of his legs.
No use of his hands.

He knows what he wants to say.
He knows how he wants to move.
He knows what he wants to hold.

All he can hold
Is time
And memory.

Syllables
To sounds
To not.

Silence.

THE DIDN'T

Hey.

Just checking in.
I hope you're doing ok.
I know there is a lot going through your head right now and it's not easy.
It's a dark hole you're down
And knowing others have been there
Brings little comfort.

It's not a competition.
You don't compare yourself to others
To justify the hurt.

But you do know
Comparison is why
You're so low.

This wasn't the plan.
This isn't the life
You thought you'd lead.

You've let yourself down.
You're trying to reconcile how you will not amount to anything
When for years, you thought you'd be something.

You thought there was something special about you.

Something unique.
Something that would shine one day.

But the sun never rose high enough
For you to sparkle,
Did it?

It's ok.
You didn't have it.
Most don't...

But you don't buy that.

You had it.
You could have amounted to something
But you didn't try, did you?

And that's what this is all about;
The reason why you are buried.
Your head clearly rotated to the back.
Looking behind at what you didn't do.

Can I say something?

You're swimming in a sea of non confidence
That can be seen a mile away
And it's ugly.

Your problem is the 180 back;
Wallowing in 'the didn't':

The roads you didn't venture down.
The effort you didn't make.
The things you didn't do.

It's self pity.
You're such a victim
And it's getting old.

That thing that would make you special,
That would make you unique...
It never went away.

You still have it
And it can still shine
But you have to do the work.

That's the hard part, isn't it?
You're scared you do the work
And there is no bloom.

It's much easier to tell yourself
You couldn't have been something
Because you didn't roll up your sleeves...
That's on you.

When the reality is
You're so fucking scared
To do the work
And have it not noticed,
Admired,
Shined upon.

What you've yet to understand
Is external admiration
Will never shine permanent light.

Their light will never reach the dark depths.

Forget giving acceptance over to others.
Give it to yourself.

Do the work for you
Create the spark.
Stoke the embers.
Feed yourself and it will blaze.

But the decider needs to be you.

You cannot change the past
But you can change the now.

Ok.
I'm going to end this here.

You are not alone and I'm here if you need me
But you have to walk this untethered.

Good night.

ONE IN THE CHAMBER

I wish Victor's place was to the east of me. I wouldn't be blinded by the rising sun right now. The glare of the ice on the highway's edge is causing me to squint so tight I wonder how I can see the road.

I follow the tarmac as it curves to the left. My squinting subsides as the glare turns to a glisten. It makes the ice and snow look alive and electric; almost an angelic glow that lulls you into the feel of lying in a large, fluffy cloud. Comfy, reclining, heaven; the opposite of my current state, which is throbbing, stiff, purgatory. The morning after the night before. In like a lamb, out like a lion.

I don't know why I didn't call her, but I didn't.

That's not true. There are many reasons I didn't call: one of them the lack of need to hear that quiet, shameful silence on the other end of the line. The disappointment I create. My self hatred is strong enough. I didn't need a mirror cast.

At times, phone silence can be clearer than your reflection. When your eyes make contact with yourself you're dealing with you and your internal dialogue; you telling you how much you've disappointed you. The silence on the other end of the line, however, tells you how much you've disappointed them, and I didn't want to hear her deafening silence again. She's put up with my bullshit for years. She loves me more than I love myself, which is easy as I made the descent from love to loathing a long time ago.

The road bends to the right. I squint in reaction and follow the white line.

I told her I'd be home early. "We'll have dinner together." I said. I told myself the same thing. I'd only have two and call it a day.

How do I fool myself each time?

I didn't tell her I'd be home early insincerely. I meant it. I believed it. When I tell myself that, I believe it... every time. And every time, the outcome is the same. Afternoon to evening to night. 2 becomes 3, 3 becomes X. I never know how many I have. My tolerance is strong and consumption is vast. I never remember the end of the beginning.

Years ago, the first drink was Russian roulette. It was a bullet in the chamber, and most nights the hammer never touched it. Last night's outcome was the minority; a one in six chance. Now, the first drink fills the cylinder. 6 bullets. 6 chambers. A sure thing. Been like that for the last while. And yet, I still believe it's a 1 in 6 chance. I still believe the outcome will be different.

It's amazing the things I tell myself.

I hear the sound of an engine. The roar as an accelerator is floored. In my rear view mirror, I see motion to the left. A pickup comes from behind, overtakes me, and eases back in line. It's hard to pass on this stretch of two lane as your view is obstructed most of the time. When you get a window to go, you need to take advantage and go.

I don't know why she doesn't go. Why would you constantly put yourself in the position of worry, anxiety, and disappointment? I believe it will be two drinks then home. She knows it won't. She knows the outcomes and yet; she stays for it. It makes me wonder if she needs my unknowing lie as much as I need the next bullet. What gives first: the immovable object or the unstoppable force?

As I approach my drive, I hesitate. My hand makes its way to the turn signal, rests on top, but I don't engage it. I pull to the shoulder of the road. The crust of the snow cracks as I decelerate. My exhale turns to frost as I sit with a downward gaze; pausing in thought as if looking for answers. There are no answers... but I can't do this like this. I'm not ready to carry the weight of the 'day after' burden. I lift my head up and scan the dash.

10:47am.

If I move it, I can make Big Mike's for opening. I'll just have two. It will help take the edge off. I'll be home mid-afternoon. We'll have dinner together. I promise.

EFFACE

Sit and I'll tell you something.
A story made to deceive.
Unsuspecting advocates.
Blind to what they see.

The weave in time.
Tightens as binds.
Unopened spine.
Proves to define.
Borders that close.
You presuppose.
Can't trust those clothes.
The story so goes.

Sit and I'll tell you something.
A reason you can't be free.
Carving their way to the future.
But the past is the vision they see.

"This is one way.
Born to obey.
Pray is I pray
Or you'll pay one day.
This ain't your place.
Don't show your face.
Hope to efface.
There's only one race."

Now I hope you tell me a story.
That my pressure will be relieved.
That all I said was bullshit.
But I find that hard to believe.

TD1

She can't.
She can't do it anymore.
Not another needle.
Not now.
Not ever.

Not another pinprick.
5 second countdown.
That she's a slave to.

Wide, vacant low.
Howl of a high.
Either eat,
Shoot,
Or stay the course.
You rarely stay the course.

So she shoots,
Pierces the skin,
Time and time again.
Skin to scar.
Scar to body.
Scar to mind.

It's not too much sugar,
Too little fiber.
It's not too much fat,

Too little exercise.
It's not of control.
Her body failed her,
Fails her.
And yet,
She failed.
She fails.

She's sick.
She's tired.
Tired of hurting her body.
Tired of fighting her body.
Tired of fighting.

She's tired.

DECIMATED

Decimated.
It comes in waves.
Before I know it,
I'm over my head.
Drowning.

I try to will it to the surface,
Bring it to life.
Needing inspiration to strike.
Now.
At this moment.

But it doesn't work that way.

So I sit with it.
That feeling of wanting:
Connection and resonance.
Consuming to the point of frustration.

It takes forever to get there
And leaves in an instant;
A hollow resolution
To a journey so long.

The act of doing
Should fulfill the wanting,
Yet it rarely does.

Why?

Why do it at all?

It will not be what I thought in my mind.
It will not provide this grand resonance
That will sweep over people
And make them wonder where it came from.

They will never know.

It lies on pages,
In files
That are not seen
Because not being able to see them
Is better than showing them
For no one to see.

It's not an act of cobbling subject and prose.

It's naked.
Transparent.
Raw.

And in the void,

It seems pointless,
Feels pointless,
Is pointless...

Until I realize

I'm the void.

FRAGILITY

If it's fragility you're worried about,
This may not be the place for you.
This is not for the faint of heart.

It's not for emotion or empathy,
Reason or virtue,
Grace or caring.

It's not for narrowing divides,
Or bridging dissent.

It's not for compassion,
Or a rising tide.
Justice,
Or the greater good.

It's what it's always been...
And it's not for me.

THE OTHER SHOE

"This is one reason I don't tell anyone about stuff like this. And I think that's sad. It's sad I can't tell anyone about the job I applied for or the girl I think I'm dating. I can't tell anyone of something I'm looking forward to because if I let anyone see it, let it see the light of day, it will be gone.

"How do you have hope living like that? How do you connect with people when you can't share something you are excited about because the act of sharing will make the possibility of it vanish, and you'll feel like a fool yet again.

"And slowly, step by step, you pull yourself from society. You pull yourself away from family and friends because you are waiting for the rug to get pulled out from under you... and you don't want to draw attention so they can watch it disappear.

"It's heartbreaking. I never wanted to be that guy, but I am that guy. I think it's all going to go away if I share it - when the reality is if I don't share it, I'm the one going away."

THE ARENA

It hurts because you were vulnerable.

It hurts because you took a chance.

You slowly unveiled yourself,
Rolled yourself out
Because there was comfort in the vulnerability.

And when there's comfort in the vulnerability,
There is no vulnerability.
That's a painful lesson.

At any moment, it can turn.
Too much of you can be too much for someone,
But not the right one.

So lick your wounds.
Pick yourself up
And brush yourself off.
Pain is progress in the arena.

CAST DEEP

He does not recognize this place.
The lines cast are deeper than before;
Pronounced and not slight.

There is no veneer
To pretty the substrate.
No change
To the die that's cast.
No sole
To heal his soul.

The allure of pretty
Is a momentary lapse of the present.
Pretty is for the young,
Not of lines cast deep.

He is of experience.
Experience has value,
Has beauty,
Has grace...
But it can never be pretty.

He lives one day at a time.
Yet, years add up at once.
His perceived connection
Was pity in disguise.

The reality of the matter
Does not really matter.

The matter brought him back to the reality
Of this place he does not recognize
With lines cast deep.

CYCLONE

She's transfixed on what she is doing wrong,
All the while, she's doing nothing wrong.
She's doing it her way, in her time.
It's her process.

She's transfixed on one intoxication flipping to another.
And the words in her head
Are a cyclone looking for dead air
That leads to peace.

She's transfixed that Kilkerran
Is being replaced by keystrokes and investigations
That leads to fixations.
The bloom and
Adulation that feeds her
Unhealthily.

She's transfixed on not doing the wrong thing
So much so, she uses the same process
That gets her the wrong things.

She's transfixed so much
That overthinking
Could cause her to overlook what's in front of her.

That thing that alludes her
Is trying to get her attention,
But it won't be seen
Until the cyclone finds the dead air.

STARS WANE

I'm trying to make it work,
Make it fit into this tight little package
Bound with a bow you'll keep as a keepsake,
As a memory of me when it was perfect,
When I was perfect.
Before the ribbon started to unravel,
And the package pulled apart at the seams.
The illusion, once luminous,
Dissolves
And the reflection back to you is gone.

I tried to make it work
So you couldn't say no.
That moments of the past were there
To flow to this.
The tears and heartbreak
Were for a purpose.
That the stars aligned
In this tight package,
Gifted when you least expected.

But stars wane.
They dim, and they burn out
Until all that's left
Is you staring into the darkness
Wondering if indeed
It was just an illusion,
A projection.
Was there ever a bow.

RANT

It's inevitable. It will happen. I'll be at a wedding, conference, dinner party when someone will ask: "Do you have kids?". I say no and then it comes... wait for it: "Are you going to have children?"

Now they could ask me for several well-meaning reasons. They could want to know more about me. They could be making conversation or they could truly care, but you know what?

Stop asking already.

I know I am 40 and not getting any younger but asking me if I'm going to have children should not be a question that bridges the gap from "What do you do for a living?" to "Can you pass the dip?"

It's a highly personal decision. My god, my mother doesn't even ask this question but some guy with a mis-buttoned shirt and a comb over has no problem dropping the question into conversation after meeting me 2 minutes prior.

Maybe I have a low sperm count.
Maybe my wife had a horrific accident and cannot conceive.
Maybe we've had 3 miscarriages.
Maybe we barely have the financial means to support ourselves.

Maybe one of our parents died of a disease that has no cure and we could not live with ourselves if we passed that gene on to our child...

Or maybe we just do not want to have children and you know what, there is nothing wrong with that.

I know it seems like an innocent question and maybe I'm being oversensitive but you would never ask someone how much money they make, or their political affiliation, or if they've accepted Jesus Christ as their personal saviour. So why would you ask them their child bearing plans?

Now I'm not saying you would ask me this question. I do not know you at all so me thinking you would ask this question could be taken as me judging you, just as asking "Are you going to have children?" can be taken the same way.

No one likes to feel that way. The world needs less judging and more compassion, less sympathy and more empathy.

So if we meet at a wedding, conference, or dinner party and I answer your first question, take a pass on the follow up and pass me the dip.

HEED THIS

Actual strength is allowing yourself to let someone in.
To seek it.
To reach for it.

Believing one can do this life in solitude is foolish.

Telling yourself you don't belong anywhere,
That you aren't connected to anything
Is self fulfilling.

You will wake up one day belonging nowhere.
You'll be alone
And down the path too far to correct it.

Changing the mindset will be impossible
Because the voice owns you.
It brainwashed you.
You don't have the strength, skill, or savvy to drown it out.

Heed this:

The most powerful thing in your life are the words you tell yourself.
They will define and access every part of your life.
You feed yourself.
Your words are your fuel,
For benefit or detriment.

Choose them wisely.

FARROW AWAY

Maybe I will astonish you.
No better outcome be true.
Though I blaze in a daze.
The craze lifts the haze
And farrows away the day.

Surrender to the beat and time.
Syncopation flows in mind.
From swing to waltz to march to fray
To quarter time past the end
And farrows away the day.

Lightning fills the skies
That scream inside my mind.
To couplets that rhyme
And nouns that define
To double to triple pentameter time.
To days to weeks to months it may stay,
Tether the hold
And farrow away the day.

Now I hope this pleases you
And once more, it pleases me too.
The creation defines,
Not a space, not a time.
It's the mindset that stays
And each morn I shall prey
As I farrow away the day.

HAD

I have a dream buried in my mind.
That our paths crossed for a moment
To meet up again over time.

That exposing my soul,
At a moment's notice
Created a bridge from then to now.

That honest confiding
And trusting my gut
Will be rewarded.

That mutual disclosures
Created a bond
Impervious and infinite.

That the value was equal:
Shared equals share.
Worth equals worthy.

That I was special.
And it was going to be
Because it is going to be.

Until I awoke one day,
Shook out the cobwebs
And realized
Had
Is all I have.

IN SILENCE

She
You know, when I thought about my future, I never pictured this.

Me
What did you picture? What did you think it would be?

She
Happier, I guess. With more clarity. I didn't really think it would be black and white, but I thought I'd have more figured out at 40 than at 29, but it doesn't feel like it. The white picket fence thing seems like it belongs more in fantasy than real life: my real life anyway

I had it. I blinked, and it all went to pieces. I couldn't put them back together because I didn't know what the picture looked like anymore. Now, I don't even know if there was a picture. It seems like some other life or alternative reality. The door closed, and it's just a haze when I look back.

I got what I wanted, then it got me.

Now I'm surrounded by people who go happily into the night. They seem like they have it all together; that they have it figured out, but they are untouched. They may know things in theory, like when you are going through a divorce - "It must be tough but it wasn't meant to be so you're better off."

That makes me want to scream.

They have no idea what a fucking failure I feel like. Everyone around me getting married and staying married. Where did I go wrong? What did I do wrong? I signed on to be a partner and wife. Now who am I?

Don't they know the hectic schedule I keep is partially done so I don't have to think. So I don't have to deal with the doubt and resentment, the decisions I made, the questions I don't have answers to. Don't pat me on the head with your downward gaze. This is not some theoretical life coming apart, it's my life!

(She pauses, takes a deep breath, closes her eyes, and slowly exhales)

I don't mean for this to come across as a pity party. I know there are many who have issues far worse than mine. And mostly, my life is pretty good. But I'm broke, emotionally broke. We all feel like that to an extent and I wish we could communicate it, talk about it, hear it, acknowledge it, recognize it, admit it, and accept it. I'm a better person because of the hurt, but god it can hurt. I'm tired of feeling like I hurt alone and in silence.

Me

But we all hurt alone and in silence.

END GAME

I thought they knew.
I thought they knew what happened;
The outcome.

I thought they knew the light they cast;
The impact that comes from
Regressive proclamations.
Not bore out of ignorance
But intent.

I thought they knew that we know them.
That this isn't a game we're buying into:
The 'bringing together to tear apart' game.

What we didn't know
Is the 'we' was getting smaller.
That 'we' were repelled to the outer edge.
That 'we' were the end game.

They knew.

THE 1 AND THE 3

I don't want this song stuck in my head.
This repeating of chorus and verse.
The 1 and the 3,
Unchanging and unending.
Loop upon loop.
Playing behind the beat
Until I'm beat.

I don't want this song stuck in my head.
The memory of which
Throws me back to that place
When I was thrown
Out of rhythm
And out of time,
Until I was out of time.

I don't want this thought stuck in my head.
Creating an illusion of a life
Coming from la la land
Connecting dots that don't exist
For pictures that never were
And mourning the loss
Of what never was.

Over present
Over thinking
Owns me.

PIGGY BACK

If you make it destructive,
Climb on my back
And point me in the direction.

Point me the opportunity
And I will skate on the euphoric high
That I know could crash me down
And burn everything around me.

But in that moment,
In that ride,
I don't care.

Implosion is what I seek.
The dizzying high
Blurring the low
And when I hit the bottom,
You call for the ride.
Let the destructive opportunity knock.

Self hatred and destruction wound in a ball.
Chasing its tail
Until the tale ends.

When this piggy back ride is over,
I'm minus the destructive
And not accepting passengers anymore.

TOMORROW

It doesn't scare me she knows,
It frightens me.

"For clarity, my interest in you is more than friends."

The sentence wasn't a question.
I could say it was a declaration,
But that seems too grand a noun to use
For a statement that began with "For clarity".

It was the beginning of a clear thought;
To state my view.

The act of being vulnerable
Is an exercise of throat gulps,
Quiet silence and
The possibility of
Not hearing your echo back.

That's a scary place.

Like you are naked on a stage,
Uplit because the moment may not end beautiful
So why show you look beautiful in the moment.

The reaction is always unknown.

It has to be.
That's how vulnerability works.
If there's comfort in the vulnerability,
There's no vulnerability.

And there is vulnerability now.

There could be agreement,
Difference,
Or indifference.

I can prospect possibilities
But only she knows the reply
At this moment in time.

Remember that.

The reply today may not be the reply tomorrow
If I made the declaration tomorrow.
I'm perfect for her today
But she may not be looking for perfect until tomorrow.
I may not be perfect then.

47th & EAU CLAIRE

Charlie sits in his car and wonders if he can go through with it. He did this once before... once. He vowed not to do it again because the experience was not pleasant, but this situation is different. It's a blind date so they must share some things in common. Pat wouldn't suggest it otherwise. It's a bit of hope, but the unknown is the unknown.

The crisp air envelops him as he makes his way to the Gaslight Diner at 47th and Eau Claire. This place has seen better days. So has Charlie.

He reaches down and turns the doorknob, squeaking as it opens inward. The floor creaks with each step. Ahead of him is a line of bar stools affixed to the floor in front of the counter. Red leatherette with chrome clad sides. The countertop is a white-flecked Arborite with the same cladding on the edge. The backsplash area has the usual items on it: a Bunn coffee maker, white cups, sea foam green milkshake mixer, glass covered pie case, and mirrors, but not in the usual setup.

There is a run of them: 2 feet wide at the top, going from end to end. In the centre, there is a mirrored 6 foot panel spanning from the countertop to the ceiling so the diners in the middle stools can look at themselves while they eat. If this place was like Chester's, guys came in here for breakfast, dinner, and occasional lunches, 7 days a week. They watch their lives pass in that mirror. The creases getting deeper, the looks more weathered, the nose... well, a little more pronounced. Why would you want you looking at you while you ate, he wonders.

To the right are 8 banquettes in a run. The benches have red leatherette, and the backing consists of wide strips of red and white material. Charlie wonders if there is some sort of law that all diners must have a red and white colour palette. Like there is a specific set of guidelines you have to follow if you want to use the word 'diner'. A trademark or copyright as such.

He feels a gaze upon him. Behind the counter, a man is slowly rotating a glass in his hand with a dishrag pushed deep to the bottom to catch every drop of water. It's a milkshake glass. The heavy hexagonal type that could survive any impact except one hurtling across the room to make a point. But there is no need to hurtle one now. His stare is making the point.

He nods his head to the left while maintaining eye contact. Charlie turns his head to the right and sees her at the last booth. At least, he assumes it's her.

His heartbeat intensifies and he can feel the weight of the moment. Why is he doing this to himself, he thinks. Sure, his life isn't great. It's not what he imagined it to be, but it is his. Does he really need the possibility of rejection to add a chill to the evening?

He makes his way to the booth.

"Elizabeth?" Charlie asks.

"Hi. Actually, I go by Elle."

"Oh, sorry. Pat said your name was Elizabeth."

"It is, legally. My mom was a fan of Elizabeth Taylor and the Queen, so it has some history. At least I have a story where it came from. I started going by Elle when I went to college. You know, wanted to make a fresh start. But Pat never got the concept and still calls me Elizabeth. That's what happens when you know someone for too long...

"I'm guessing you're Charlie? Please say yes. This is a tad awkward otherwise."

"I'm Charlie. Nice to meet you, Elle."

"Nice to meet you too, Charlie."

He takes his coat off and slips into the booth. A glimmer catches his eye, and he notices a heart-shaped pendant on her necklace.

"That's beautiful." He says.

"What?"

"Your necklace. It's beautiful. Very graceful."

"Oh, thank you. My mother gave it to me. It's the same as Elizabeth Montgomery wore on Bewitched. Another Elizabeth I was named after. I never liked the show but my mom was a fan. She said their love was idyllic. How they braved the storm and never let it tear them apart... I always found it a prime example of how a woman suppresses who she is for a man." Elle pauses for a moment and slowly closes her eyes. "Sorry. That was a bit negative, wasn't it?"

"No, I don't think so. You like what you like. Nothing wrong with that and you don't have to apologize for it." Charlie turns his head and does a quick survey of the room. "It's quiet for a Friday night."

"We are always quiet this time of night. We've closed."

" 'We're closed?' Do you work here?"

"I do, and I own it; though sometimes I feel like it owns me." Elle looks to her right to the man behind the counter. "Edgar, could you bring us 2 coffees. Is coffee ok, Charlie?"

"I'll take a club soda, if you have it."

"Of course. Edgar..." Before she can finish her sentence, Edgar nods and brings over the drinks. "Thank you." Elle stirs her coffee and takes a sip. "Me owning this place was a natural, but somewhat unwanted, progression. It's been in the family for generations. My great-great-great-great-grandfather opened it. It's had one name, been in 2 towns, seen 29 presidents, 23 prime ministers, 10 Popes, 4 James Bonds, and now I'm at the helm of the ship."

"Who's your favourite James Bond?"
"Lazenby. I thought you were going to ask who is my favourite Pope."

"Does anyone have a favourite Pope?"

"I do, but more along the lines of most interesting than favourite... now that I think of it, I have 2. Benedict IX was Pope three times. He actually sold the papacy to end his second go around. The second is Pope John, who served around 855 AD. The rumour was that John was a Joan and gave birth while Pope."

"You know a lot about Popes."

"It was one of my areas of study in school. I wasn't raised religious but always been interested in the Catholic Church. I can't say where it comes from, but a billion people can't be wrong, can they? Your look suggests otherwise Charlie... and disapproval."

"No, no. No disapproval. It's just not for me, that's all. I was raised Catholic, was an alter boy, taught by nuns, the full experience. When I was young, I thought I would be a priest, but the nuns beat that out of me."

"Ah, a bitter, lapsed Catholic, I see."

"Who's disapproving now," he says with a coy smile. "I'm not bitter. I'm glad I was raised in the faith. It gave me structure I appreciate today. And it gave me a love of the structures that house it. Some of the greatest architecture around are older churches." Charlie twists his glass with his left hand. "Plus, it gave me endless guilt and a fine sense of humour. But I've moved on from the whole smoke and mirrors, Holy Spirit thing."

"Fair enough." Elle takes a sip of coffee that begins a quiet moment between them. Charlie breaks the silence.

"Lazenby... if the Pope conversation happened before the Bond question, I'd have called that fore-shadowing."

"What can I say? I like the underdog, Charlie. Tell me, are you always this sarcastic?"

"I reserve it for conversations with 6th generation diner owners."

HOLD TIGHT

In this crazy, uncertain world, don't forget

Stars need to be touched.
Mountains need to be climbed.
Dreams need to flourish.

Hold tight & reach hard

WITH THANKS

Big shout out to Nicola MacNeil for the amazing collage on the cover. It is beyond perfect and I appreciate the thought, dedication, and care you put into its creation.

I owe a huge debt of gratitude to Alex Baisley. This book would not exist without you. Full stop. Your support, thoughtful feedback, and encouragement guided me along a path I didn't know existed. Thank you for helping me achieve my big dream. You most certainly are my long suffering editor (chapeau to Stuart McLean).

I'm grateful for the challenges put in front of me and the amazing people I crossed paths with over the years. This book would not exist without the following:

Covid Reaper
Jib Jab
Eve of the Eve
Elliot Lake
Pecan Nonsense
Waving Pineapples
Bistro 164
Second Cup
Galveston
Goderich
Cadence
1229 Sheffield

3rd and San Vicente
Strange Guelph News
IMAP

Thank you for taking time out of your day to read my attempt at writing a book. If you'd like to say hi, you can find me on Instagram @Darrell_k or drop me a note Darrell@atlanticwaypublishing.com

All the best,

Darrell

www.ingramcontent.com/pod-product-compliance
Lightning Source LLC
Chambersburg PA
CBHW030457010526
44118CB00011B/981